This book belongs to:

_____

Starting Balance _____

Transaction Codes
DD - Direct Debit   ATM - Cash Withdrawal
CC - Credit Card   DC - Debit Card   C - Cheque

Date	Code/Number	Description of transaction	Incoming	Outgoing	Balance

Starting Balance _____

Transaction Codes

DD - Direct Debit   ATM - Cash Withdrawal

CC - Credit Card   DC - Debit Card   C - Cheque

Date	Code/ Number	Description of transaction	Incoming	Outgoing	Balance

Starting Balance _____

Transaction Codes

DD - Direct Debit   ATM - Cash Withdrawal
CC - Credit Card   DC - Debit Card   C - Cheque

Date	Code/Number	Description of transaction	Incoming	Outgoing	Balance

Starting Balance _____

Transaction Codes

DD - Direct Debit   ATM - Cash Withdrawal
CC - Credit Card   DC - Debit Card   C - Cheque

Date	Code/Number	Description of transaction	Incoming	Outgoing	Balance

Starting Balance _____

Transaction Codes DD - Direct Debit ATM - Cash Withdrawal
  CC - Credit Card DC - Debit Card C - Cheque

Date	Code/Number	Description of transaction	Incoming	Outgoing	Balance

Starting Balance _____

Transaction Codes

DD - Direct Debit ATM - Cash Withdrawal
CC - Credit Card DC - Debit Card C - Cheque

Date	Code/Number	Description of transaction	Incoming	Outgoing	Balance

Starting Balance _____

Transaction Codes
DD - Direct Debit   ATM - Cash Withdrawal
CC - Credit Card   DC - Debit Card   C - Cheque

Date	Code/Number	Description of transaction	Incoming	Outgoing	Balance

Starting Balance _____

Transaction Codes

DD - Direct Debit   ATM - Cash Withdrawal
CC - Credit Card   DC - Debit Card   C - Cheque

Date	Code/Number	Description of transaction	Incoming	Outgoing	Balance

Starting Balance _____

Transaction Codes

DD - Direct Debit   ATM - Cash Withdrawal
CC - Credit Card   DC - Debit Card   C - Cheque

Date	Code/Number	Description of transaction	Incoming	Outgoing	Balance

Starting Balance _____

Transaction Codes

DD - Direct Debit   ATM - Cash Withdrawal
CC - Credit Card   DC - Debit Card   C - Cheque

Date	Code/ Number	Description of transaction	Incoming	Outgoing	Balance

Starting Balance _____

Transaction Codes   DD - Direct Debit   ATM - Cash Withdrawal
    CC - Credit Card   DC - Debit Card   C - Cheque

Date	Code/Number	Description of transaction	Incoming	Outgoing	Balance

Starting Balance _____

Transaction Codes

DD - Direct Debit ATM - Cash Withdrawal
CC - Credit Card DC - Debit Card C - Cheque

Date	Code/Number	Description of transaction	Incoming	Outgoing	Balance

Starting Balance _____

Transaction Codes DD - Direct Debit   ATM - Cash Withdrawal
CC - Credit Card   DC - Debit Card   C - Cheque

Date	Code/Number	Description of transaction	Incoming	Outgoing	Balance

Starting Balance _____

Transaction Codes

DD - Direct Debit   ATM - Cash Withdrawal
CC - Credit Card   DC - Debit Card   C - Cheque

Date	Code/Number	Description of transaction	Incoming	Outgoing	Balance

Starting Balance _____

Transaction Codes

DD - Direct Debit   ATM - Cash Withdrawal
CC - Credit Card   DC - Debit Card   C - Cheque

Date	Code/Number	Description of transaction	Incoming	Outgoing	Balance

Starting Balance _____

Transaction Codes DD - Direct Debit   ATM - Cash Withdrawal
CC - Credit Card   DC - Debit Card   C - Cheque

Date	Code/Number	Description of transaction	Incoming	Outgoing	Balance

Starting Balance _____

Transaction Codes
- DD - Direct Debit
- ATM - Cash Withdrawal
- CC - Credit Card
- DC - Debit Card
- C - Cheque

Date	Code/Number	Description of transaction	Incoming	Outgoing	Balance

Starting Balance _____

Transaction Codes   DD - Direct Debit   ATM - Cash Withdrawal
                       CC - Credit Card   DC - Debit Card   C - Cheque

Date	Code/ Number	Description of transaction	Incoming	Outgoing	Balance

Starting Balance _____

Transaction DD - Direct Debit   ATM - Cash Withdrawal
Codes   CC - Credit Card   DC - Debit Card   C - Cheque

Date	Code/ Number	Description of transaction	Incoming	Outgoing	Balance

Starting Balance _____

Transaction Codes

DD - Direct Debit ATM - Cash Withdrawal
CC - Credit Card   DC - Debit Card   C - Cheque

Date	Code/Number	Description of transaction	Incoming	Outgoing	Balance

Starting Balance _____

Transaction Codes   DD - Direct Debit   ATM - Cash Withdrawal
                           CC - Credit Card   DC - Debit Card   C - Cheque

Date	Code/Number	Description of transaction	Incoming	Outgoing	Balance

Starting Balance _____

Transaction Codes   DD - Direct Debit   ATM - Cash Withdrawal
                     CC - Credit Card   DC - Debit Card   C - Cheque

Date	Code/Number	Description of transaction	Incoming	Outgoing	Balance

Starting Balance _____

Transaction Codes

DD - Direct Debit   ATM - Cash Withdrawal
CC - Credit Card   DC - Debit Card   C - Cheque

Date	Code/Number	Description of transaction	Incoming	Outgoing	Balance

Starting Balance _____

Transaction Codes DD - Direct Debit   ATM - Cash W thdrawal
CC - Credit Card   DC - Debit Card   C - Cheque

Date	Code/ Number	Description of transaction	Incoming	Outgoing	Balance

Starting Balance _____

Transaction Codes   DD - Direct Debit   ATM - Cash Withdrawal
                    CC - Credit Card   DC - Debit Card   C - Cheque

Date	Code/Number	Description of transaction	Incoming	Outgoing	Balance

Starting Balance _____

Transaction Codes

DD - Direct Debit ATM - Cash Withdrawal
CC - Credit Card DC - Debit Card C - Cheque

Date	Code/Number	Description of transaction	Incoming	Outgoing	Balance

Starting Balance _____

Transaction Codes   DD - Direct Debit   ATM - Cash Withdrawal
                       CC - Credit Card   DC - Debit Card   C - Cheque

Date	Code/Number	Description of transaction	Incoming	Outgoing	Balance

Starting Balance _____

Transaction Codes

DD - Direct Debit   ATM - Cash Withdrawal
CC - Credit Card   DC - Debit Card   C - Cheque

Date	Code/Number	Description of transaction	Incoming	Outgoing	Balance

Starting Balance _____

Transaction Codes

DD - Direct Debit   ATM - Cash Withdrawal
CC - Credit Card   DC - Debit Card   C - Cheque

Date	Code/Number	Description of transaction	Incoming	Outgoing	Balance

Starting Balance _____

Transaction Codes

DD - Direct Debit   ATM - Cash Withdrawal
CC - Credit Card   DC - Debit Card   C - Cheque

Date	Code/Number	Description of transaction	Incoming	Outgoing	Balance

Starting Balance _____

Transaction Codes   DD - Direct Debit   ATM - Cash Withdrawal
CC - Credit Card   DC - Debit Card   C - Cheque

Date	Code/Number	Description of transaction	Incoming	Outgoing	Balance

Starting Balance _____

Transaction Codes   DD - Direct Debit   ATM - Cash Withdrawal
                     CC - Credit Card   DC - Debit Card   C - Cheque

Date	Code/Number	Description of transaction	Incoming	Outgoing	Balance

Starting Balance _____

Transaction Codes
DD - Direct Debit   ATM - Cash Withdrawal
CC - Credit Card   DC - Debit Card   C - Cheque

Date	Code/Number	Description of transaction	Incoming	Outgoing	Balance

Starting Balance _____

Transaction Codes

DD - Direct Debit   ATM - Cash Withdrawal
CC - Credit Card   DC - Debit Card   C - Cheque

Date	Code/Number	Description of transaction	Incoming	Outgoing	Balance

Starting Balance _____

Transaction Codes

DD - Direct Debit   ATM - Cash Withdrawal
CC - Credit Card   DC - Debit Card   C - Cheque

Date	Code/Number	Description of transaction	Incoming	Outgoing	Balance

Starting Balance _____

Transaction   DD - Direct Debit   ATM - Cash Withdrawal
   Codes   CC - Credit Card   DC - Debit Card   C - Cheque

Date	Code/ Number	Description of transaction	Incoming	Outgoing	Balance

Starting Balance _____

Transaction Codes   DD - Direct Debit   ATM - Cash Withdrawal
                     CC - Credit Card   DC - Debit Card   C - Cheque

Date	Code/Number	Description of transaction	Incoming	Outgoing	Balance

Starting Balance _____

Transaction Codes
DD - Direct Debit   ATM - Cash Withdrawal
CC - Credit Card   DC - Debit Card   C - Cheque

Date	Code/Number	Description of transaction	Incoming	Outgoing	Balance

Starting Balance _____

Transaction Codes

DD - Direct Debit   ATM - Cash Withdrawal
CC - Credit Card   DC - Debit Card   C - Cheque

Date	Code/Number	Description of transaction	Incoming	Outgoing	Balance

Starting Balance _____

Transaction Codes

DD - Direct Debit   ATM - Cash Withdrawal
CC - Credit Card   DC - Debit Card   C - Cheque

Date	Code/Number	Description of transaction	Incoming	Outgoing	Balance

Starting Balance _____

Transaction Codes

DD - Direct Debit   ATM - Cash Withdrawal
CC - Credit Card   DC - Debit Card   C - Cheque

Date	Code/Number	Description of transaction	Incoming	Outgoing	Balance

Starting Balance _____

Transaction Codes   DD - Direct Debit   ATM - Cash Withdrawal
                      CC - Credit Card   DC - Debit Card   C - Cheque

Date	Code/Number	Description of transaction	Incoming	Outgoing	Balance

Starting Balance _____

Transaction Codes: DD - Direct Debit   ATM - Cash Withdrawal   CC - Credit Card   DC - Debit Card   C - Cheque

Date	Code/Number	Description of transaction	Incoming	Outgoing	Balance

Starting Balance _____

Transaction Codes   DD - Direct Debit   ATM - Cash Withdrawal
                         CC - Credit Card   DC - Debit Card   C - Cheque

Date	Code/Number	Description of transaction	Incoming	Outgoing	Balance

Starting Balance _____

Transaction Codes

DD - Direct Debit   ATM - Cash Withdrawal
CC - Credit Card   DC - Debit Card   C - Cheque

Date	Code/Number	Description of transaction	Incoming	Outgoing	Balance

Starting Balance _____

Transaction Codes

DD - Direct Debit   ATM - Cash Withdrawal
CC - Credit Card   DC - Debit Card   C - Cheque

Date	Code/Number	Description of transaction	Incoming	Outgoing	Balance

Starting Balance _____

Transaction Codes

DD - Direct Debit   ATM - Cash Withdrawal
CC - Credit Card   DC - Debit Card   C - Cheque

Date	Code/Number	Description of transaction	Incoming	Outgoing	Balance

Starting Balance _____

Transaction Codes   DD - Direct Debit   ATM - Cash Withdrawal
                     CC - Credit Card   DC - Debit Card   C - Cheque

Date	Code/Number	Description of transaction	Incoming	Outgoing	Balance

Starting Balance _____

Transaction Codes　　DD - Direct Debit　ATM - Cash Withdrawal
　　　　　　　　　　CC - Credit Card　DC - Debit Card　C - Cheque

Date	Code/Number	Description of transaction	Incoming	Outgoing	Balance

Starting Balance _____

Transaction Codes

DD - Direct Debit   ATM - Cash Withdrawal
CC - Credit Card   DC - Debit Card   C - Cheque

Date	Code/Number	Description of transaction	Incoming	Outgoing	Balance

Starting Balance _____

Transaction Codes

DD - Direct Debit   ATM - Cash Withdrawal
CC - Credit Card   DC - Debit Card   C - Cheque

Date	Code/Number	Description of transaction	Incoming	Outgoing	Balance

Starting Balance _____

Transaction Codes   DD - Direct Debit   ATM - Cash Withdrawal
                     CC - Credit Card   DC - Debit Card   C - Cheque

Date	Code/Number	Description of transaction	Incoming	Outgoing	Balance

Starting Balance _____

Transaction Codes

DD - Direct Debit   ATM - Cash Withdrawal
CC - Credit Card   DC - Debit Card   C - Cheque

Date	Code/Number	Description of transaction	Incoming	Outgoing	Balance

Starting Balance _____

Transaction Codes   DD - Direct Debit   ATM - Cash Withdrawal
                       CC - Credit Card   DC - Debit Card   C - Cheque

Date	Code/ Number	Description of transaction	Incoming	Outgoing	Balance

Starting Balance _____

Transaction Codes   DD - Direct Debit   ATM - Cash Withdrawal
CC - Credit Card   DC - Debit Card   C - Cheque

Date	Code/Number	Description of transaction	Incoming	Outgoing	Balance

Starting Balance _____

Transaction Codes

DD - Direct Debit   ATM - Cash Withdrawal
CC - Credit Card   DC - Debit Card   C - Cheque

Date	Code/Number	Description of transaction	Incoming	Outgoing	Balance

Starting Balance _____

Transaction Codes DD - Direct Debit   ATM - Cash Withdrawal
             CC - Credit Card   DC - Debit Card   C - Cheque

Date	Code/Number	Description of transaction	Incoming	Outgoing	Balance

Starting Balance _____

Transaction Codes
- DD - Direct Debit
- ATM - Cash Withdrawal
- CC - Credit Card
- DC - Debit Card
- C - Cheque

Date	Code/Number	Description of transaction	Incoming	Outgoing	Balance

Starting Balance _____

Transaction Codes   DD - Direct Debit   ATM - Cash Withdrawal
                       CC - Credit Card   DC - Debit Card   C - Cheque

Date	Code/Number	Description of transaction	Incoming	Outgoing	Balance

Starting Balance _____

Transaction Codes   DD - Direct Debit   ATM - Cash W thdrawal
                       CC - Credit Card   DC - Debit Card   C - Cheque

Date	Code/Number	Description of transaction	Incoming	Outgoing	Balance

Starting Balance _____

Transaction Codes
DD - Direct Debit   ATM - Cash Withdrawal
CC - Credit Card   DC - Debit Card   C - Cheque

Date	Code/Number	Description of transaction	Incoming	Outgoing	Balance

Starting Balance _____

Transaction Codes
DD - Direct Debit   ATM - Cash Withdrawal
CC - Credit Card   DC - Debit Card   C - Cheque

Date	Code/Number	Description of transaction	Incoming	Outgoing	Balance

Starting Balance _____

Transaction Codes

DD - Direct Debit   ATM - Cash Withdrawal
CC - Credit Card   DC - Debit Card   C - Cheque

Date	Code/Number	Description of transaction	Incoming	Outgoing	Balance

Starting Balance _____

Transaction Codes

DD - Direct Debit   ATM - Cash Withdrawal
CC - Credit Card   DC - Debit Card   C - Cheque

Date	Code/Number	Description of transaction	Incoming	Outgoing	Balance

Starting Balance _____

Transaction Codes   DD - Direct Debit   ATM - Cash Withdrawal
    CC - Credit Card   DC - Debit Card   C - Cheque

Date	Code/Number	Description of transaction	Incoming	Outgoing	Balance

Starting Balance _____

Transaction Codes

DD - Direct Debit   ATM - Cash W thdrawal
CC - Credit Card   DC - Debit Card   C - Cheque

Date	Code/Number	Description of transaction	Incoming	Outgoing	Balance

Starting Balance _____

Transaction Codes   DD - Direct Debit   ATM - Cash Withdrawal
                     CC - Credit Card   DC - Debit Card   C - Cheque

Date	Code/ Number	Description of transaction	Incoming	Outgoing	Balance

Starting Balance _____

Transaction Codes

DD - Direct Debit   ATM - Cash Withdrawal
CC - Credit Card   DC - Debit Card   C - Cheque

Date	Code/Number	Description of transaction	Incoming	Outgoing	Balance

Starting Balance _____

Transaction Codes

DD - Direct Debit   ATM - Cash Withdrawal
CC - Credit Card   DC - Debit Card   C - Cheque

Date	Code/Number	Description of transaction	Incoming	Outgoing	Balance

Starting Balance _____

Transaction Codes

DD - Direct Debit   ATM - Cash Withdrawal
CC - Credit Card   DC - Debit Card   C - Cheque

Date	Code/Number	Description of transaction	Incoming	Outgoing	Balance

Starting Balance _____

Transaction Codes
DD - Direct Debit   ATM - Cash Withdrawal
CC - Credit Card   DC - Debit Card   C - Cheque

Date	Code/Number	Description of transaction	Incoming	Outgoing	Balance

Starting Balance _____

Transaction Codes

DD - Direct Debit   ATM - Cash Withdrawal
CC - Credit Card   DC - Debit Card   C - Cheque

Date	Code/ Number	Description of transaction	Incoming	Outgoing	Balance

Starting Balance _____

Transaction Codes   DD - Direct Debit   ATM - Cash Withdrawal
                        CC - Credit Card   DC - Debit Card   C - Cheque

Date	Code/Number	Description of transaction	Incoming	Outgoing	Balance

Starting Balance _____

Transaction Codes DD - Direct Debit   ATM - Cash Withdrawal
                   CC - Credit Card   DC - Debit Card   C - Cheque

Date	Code/Number	Description of transaction	Incoming	Outgoing	Balance

Starting Balance _____

Transaction Codes   DD - Direct Debit   ATM - Cash Withdrawal
                     CC - Credit Card   DC - Debit Card   C - Cheque

Date	Code/Number	Description of transaction	Incoming	Outgoing	Balance

Starting Balance _____

Transaction Codes

DD - Direct Debit   ATM - Cash Withdrawal
CC - Credit Card   DC - Debit Card   C - Cheque

Date	Code/Number	Description of transaction	Incoming	Outgoing	Balance

Starting Balance _____

Transaction Codes

DD - Direct Debit   ATM - Cash Withdrawal
CC - Credit Card   DC - Debit Card   C - Cheque

Date	Code/Number	Description of transaction	Incoming	Outgoing	Balance

Starting Balance _____

Transaction Codes

DD - Direct Debit   ATM - Cash Withdrawal
CC - Credit Card   DC - Debit Card   C - Cheque

Date	Code/Number	Description of transaction	Incoming	Outgoing	Balance

Starting Balance _____

Transaction Codes   DD - Direct Debit   ATM - Cash Withdrawal
                           CC - Credit Card   DC - Debit Card   C - Cheque

Date	Code/Number	Description of transaction	Incoming	Outgoing	Balance

Starting Balance _____

Transaction Codes

DD - Direct Debit   ATM - Cash Withdrawal
CC - Credit Card   DC - Debit Card   C - Cheque

Date	Code/Number	Description of transaction	Incoming	Outgoing	Balance

Starting Balance _____

Transaction Codes

DD - Direct Debit   ATM - Cash Withdrawal
CC - Credit Card   DC - Debit Card   C - Cheque

Date	Code/Number	Description of transaction	Incoming	Outgoing	Balance

Starting Balance _____

Transaction Codes

DD - Direct Debit   ATM - Cash Withdrawal
CC - Credit Card   DC - Debit Card   C - Cheque

Date	Code/ Number	Description of transaction	Incoming	Outgoing	Balance

Starting Balance _____

Transaction Codes

DD - Direct Debit   ATM - Cash Withdrawal
CC - Credit Card   DC - Debit Card   C - Cheque

Date	Code/Number	Description of transaction	Incoming	Outgoing	Balance

Starting Balance _____

Transaction Codes

DD - Direct Debit   ATM - Cash Withdrawal
CC - Credit Card   DC - Debit Card   C - Cheque

Date	Code/Number	Description of transaction	Incoming	Outgoing	Balance

Starting Balance _____

Transaction Codes DD - Direct Debit   ATM - Cash Withdrawal
CC - Credit Card   DC - Debit Card   C - Cheque

Date	Code/ Number	Description of transaction	Incoming	Outgoing	Balance

Starting Balance _____

Transaction Codes   DD - Direct Debit   ATM - Cash Withdrawal
CC - Credit Card   DC - Debit Card   C - Cheque

Date	Code/Number	Description of transaction	Incoming	Outgoing	Balance

Starting Balance _____

Transaction Codes   DD - Direct Debit   ATM - Cash Withdrawal
                      CC - Credit Card   DC - Debit Card   C - Cheque

Date	Code/Number	Description of transaction	Incoming	Outgoing	Balance

Starting Balance _____

Transaction Codes
DD - Direct Debit   ATM - Cash Withdrawal
CC - Credit Card   DC - Debit Card   C - Cheque

Date	Code/Number	Description of transaction	Incoming	Outgoing	Balance

Starting Balance _____

Transaction Codes

DD - Direct Debit   ATM - Cash Withdrawal
CC - Credit Card   DC - Debit Card   C - Cheque

Date	Code/Number	Description of transaction	Incoming	Outgoing	Balance

Starting Balance _____

Transaction Codes

DD - Direct Debit   ATM - Cash Withdrawal
CC - Credit Card   DC - Debit Card   C - Cheque

Date	Code/Number	Description of transaction	Incoming	Outgoing	Balance

Starting Balance _____

Transaction Codes   DD - Direct Debit   ATM - Cash Withdrawal
                     CC - Credit Card   DC - Debit Card   C - Cheque

Date	Code/Number	Description of transaction	Incoming	Outgoing	Balance

Starting Balance _____

Transaction Codes

DD - Direct Debit   ATM - Cash Withdrawal
CC - Credit Card   DC - Debit Card   C - Cheque

Date	Code/ Number	Description of transaction	Incoming	Outgoing	Balance

Starting Balance _____

Transaction Codes
DD - Direct Debit   ATM - Cash Withdrawal
CC - Credit Card   DC - Debit Card   C - Cheque

Date	Code/Number	Description of transaction	Incoming	Outgoing	Balance

Starting Balance _____

Transaction Codes   DD - Direct Debit   ATM - Cash Withdrawal   CC - Credit Card   DC - Debit Card   C - Cheque

Date	Code/Number	Description of transaction	Incoming	Outgoing	Balance

Starting Balance _____

Transaction Codes   DD - Direct Debit   ATM - Cash Withdrawal
    CC - Credit Card   DC - Debit Card   C - Cheque

Date	Code/Number	Description of transaction	Incoming	Outgoing	Balance

Starting Balance _____

Transaction Codes

DD - Direct Debit   ATM - Cash Withdrawal
CC - Credit Card   DC - Debit Card   C - Cheque

Date	Code/Number	Description of transaction	Incoming	Outgoing	Balance

Starting Balance _____

Transaction Codes   DD - Direct Debit   ATM - Cash Withdrawal   CC - Credit Card   DC - Debit Card   C - Cheque

Date	Code/Number	Description of transaction	Incoming	Outgoing	Balance

Starting Balance _____

Transaction Codes

DD - Direct Debit   ATM - Cash Withdrawal
CC - Credit Card   DC - Debit Card   C - Cheque

Date	Code/Number	Description of transaction	Incoming	Outgoing	Balance

Starting Balance _____

Transaction Codes DD - Direct Debit ATM - Cash Withdrawal
CC - Credit Card DC - Debit Card C - Cheque

Date	Code/Number	Description of transaction	Incoming	Outgoing	Balance

Starting Balance _____

Transaction Codes

DD - Direct Debit   ATM - Cash Withdrawal
CC - Credit Card   DC - Debit Card   C - Cheque

Date	Code/Number	Description of transaction	Incoming	Outgoing	Balance

Starting Balance _____

Transaction Codes

DD - Direct Debit ATM - Cash Withdrawal
CC - Credit Card DC - Debit Card C - Cheque

Date	Code/Number	Description of transaction	Incoming	Outgoing	Balance

Starting Balance _____

Transaction Codes

DD - Direct Debit   ATM - Cash Withdrawal
CC - Credit Card   DC - Debit Card   C - Cheque

Date	Code/ Number	Description of transaction	Incoming	Outgoing	Balance

Starting Balance _____

Transaction Codes
DD - Direct Debit ATM - Cash Withdrawal
CC - Credit Card DC - Debit Card C - Cheque

Date	Code/Number	Description of transaction	Incoming	Outgoing	Balance

Starting Balance _____

Transaction Codes

DD - Direct Debit   ATM - Cash Withdrawal
CC - Credit Card   DC - Debit Card   C - Cheque

Date	Code/ Number	Description of transaction	Incoming	Outgoing	Balance

www.ingramcontent.com/pod-product-compliance
Lightning Source LLC
Chambersburg PA
CBHW070424220526
45466CB00004B/1535